# Things
# Natural, Wild,
# and Free

## The Life of Aldo Leopold

# Marybeth Lorbiecki

FULCRUM
GOLDEN, COLORADO

*For Nina Leopold Bradley, who–like her father, mother, and siblings–has dedicated so much of her life to caring for things natural, wild, and free, showing others how to do the same. I'm so grateful for your model and friendship. You have given the world more than can be measured. (1917–2011)*

My gratitude to Nina Leopold Bradley, for sharing loving memories of her father and giving me access to family papers and photographs; Curt Meine, who introduced me to Aldo, inspired me to write this book, and served as a resource along the way; Sam Scinta, Carolyn Sobczak, and Jack Lenzo from Fulcrum Publishing; Buddy Huffaker from The Aldo Leopold Foundation; Robert A. McCabe; Art Hawkins; Bernie Schermetzler of the University of Wisconsin Archives; Stephen Brower; Betty Beck and Helen Parsons of the Des Moines County Historical Society; Gaylord Nelson.

Note: Aldo's real name was Rand Aldo Leopold. While he was still an infant, his family dropped "Rand" from his name.

Text © 2011 by Marybeth Lorbiecki
Photographs used with permission of The Aldo Leopold Foundation: 2, 4, 5, 7, 9, 10, 11, 14, 17, 20, 26, 29, 31, 33, 34, 38, 45, 47, 50, 54, 55, 59, 61, 66, 71, 72, 73, 75, 76, 77, 79, 83, 84, 91, 92, 93. Photograph courtesy of the Forest History Society, Durham, NC: front cover, i, 24 (J. D. Guthrie, for the US Forest Service). Photograph courtesy of The Lawrenceville School: 15. Photographs courtesy of the Library of Congress, Prints and Photographs Division: 42 (LC-USZ62-124387), 62 (FSA/OWI Collection, LC-USF33-000067-M3). Photograph courtesy of Jon Lee: 69. Cover image by permission of Oxford University Press, Inc.: 88, (OUP, 1968). Photograph by Marybeth Lorbiecki: 89.

Library of Congress Cataloging-in-Publication Data
Lorbiecki, Marybeth.
  Things natural, wild, and free : the life of Aldo Leopold / Marybeth Lorbiecki.
    p. cm. -- (Conservation adventurers)
  Includes bibliographical references and index.
  ISBN 978-1-55591-474-5 (pbk.)
  1. Leopold, Aldo, 1886-1948--Juvenile literature. 2. Naturalists--Wisconsin--Biography--Juvenile literature. 3. Conservationists--Wisconsin--Biography--Juvenile literature. I. Title.
  QH31.L618L676 2011
  333.95'16092--dc23
  [B]
                          2011019999

Printed in Canada
0 9 8 7 6 5 4 3 2 1

Design by Jack Lenzo

Fulcrum Publishing
4690 Table Mountain Dr., Ste. 100
Golden, CO 80403
800-992-2908 · 303-277-1623
www.fulcrumbooks.com

# Contents

# Foreword

Have you ever canoed over wild water, camped in the woods, or watched a bird do a courting dance? Or maybe you've seen raccoon tracks in your yard or caught a big fish.

These are just some of the adventures Aldo Leopold enjoyed from the time he was a kid. He loved the outdoors so much that he decided to make protecting it his life's work. And because he did, we have the wild animals and places he helped conserve and preserve.

As a kid, I spent most of my time outdoors barefoot. I always had dirty feet, but I didn't care. I loved the feel of fresh-cut grass between my toes. I liked helping my mother garden, and some of my best memories were at my grandmother's farm. It was a special place where I'd roam the woods from sunup to sundown. I'd pack a picnic lunch and retreat to a fort we kids made along the creek. We'd spend the day swimming, collecting bugs and frogs and letting them go, and tracking animals. Like young Aldo, we were like detectives trying to solve a mystery—what animal made that print or what creatures left behind their fur, feathers, or scat? We had to find out!

These experiences led me to my career teaching

outdoor education to people across the country. I get to show others how fun and exciting it is to explore nature.

As you follow Aldo's life, think about some of your own outdoor adventures. Aldo hoped that people would learn to love the land, and to love it, we must be in it, enjoying it. So take some time, go outdoors, and explore it all. Find that special place that makes you happy (like my grandmother's farm). Learn about all the animals, birds, fish, and plants that share it with you, and find ways to take care of them. You can organize a habitat project or a cleanup day, or build a bench so that others can share your special place. Whatever you choose, remember to respect these areas for others to experience in the future.

Who knows, someday it might be your kids who visit the land you love! Until then, go outside and see what you can discover and what fun you can have, too, as you learn to "read the land," just like Aldo.

–Janine Kohn,
National program coordinator,
Pheasants Forever's Leopold Education Project

# 1
# Woodscraft and Honor

Eight-year-old Aldo Leopold walked along the path, trying not to rustle the leaves. Suddenly his father, Carl, stopped and flipped a rotting log. Spud barked excitedly. Underneath the log was a tuft of brown fur, a trail of slender paw prints, and a pile of crayfish skeletons. What had lived here?

By the look of the prints, a mink.

Aldo's father could read stories from the land like other people could read them out of books. Carl had once been a traveling salesman. He had journeyed over the midwestern territories by buckboard and by foot, selling barbed wire and roller skates. He had hunted, camped, and lived off the land. Now at each Sunday picnic, Carl led his children on nature walks to teach them the ways of the woods, prairies, and swamps.

Aldo absorbed his father's words. He asked question after question and dreamed of living his father's adventures.

On Saturdays, while his father was out hunting, Aldo would cross the yard to the Big House. There lived his German grandparents, Opa and Oma Starker. Their mansion crowned Prospect Hill, overlooking the

Aldo totes his stick rifle as he walks with his younger brother
Carl and his father, Carl Leopold, on the way to their day's
adventure at the Crystal Lake Hunt Club.

Mississippi River and Burlington, Iowa.

Opa had come from Germany as a young architect and landscape engineer. Over the years, he had become one of Burlington's most successful businessmen. He'd designed buildings and run a grocery company, bank, and other businesses. All the while, he loved music, arts, and the natural world. He helped Burlington build a free public library and an opera house. He also worked to preserve land in Crapo Park (the city named a lake in it after him). Now retired, he tended his gardens and his grandchildren. Aldo would trail after Opa, learning how to grow trees, flowers, and vegetables. Opa spoke German and always carried his pruning shears in his pocket. Each year he recruited Aldo and his family to help with his spring planting, when he transformed his yard into a lush bluffside park.

Born January 11, 1887, Aldo was the oldest of the Leopold children. He led his siblings–Marie and his brothers, Carl and little Frederick–on escapades. They skated on the river, trapped rabbits, and collected plants. There were riotous snowball fights and free-for-all baseball games. At night, the Leopolds would gather in the Starker parlor. The gas lamps flickered in huge mirrors as Aldo's mother, Clara, played the piano and everyone sang. The smell of

Aldo (upper left) poses with his mother, Clara Starker Leopold, Maria, Frederick, and Carl Jr. (clockwise around Clara)
about 1901.

German pastries hung in the air. Possessed by a lively sweet tooth, Aldo would snitch treats when no one was looking.

When Aldo started school, he could speak both English and German. He excelled in his classes but liked exploring better. He and his Irish spaniel, Spud, would take off to examine the riverbanks, the bluffs, and the sloughs. Black Hawk Cave and Starr's Cave offered cool, bat-winged tunnels to crawl through and springs to drink from. Sometimes Aldo got so caught up in his adventures, he skipped school.

Starr's Cave, with its limestone cliffs, was one of Aldo's favorite destinations for bird-watching and exploring. A park now preserves these haunts.

A steady stream of traffic flowed back and forth below Aldo's home on the bluff. Tugboats guided enormous log rafts, and steamboats carried well-dressed passengers. Overhead, flocks of migrating birds flew north or south, depending on the season. Birds were Aldo's specialty. At eleven, he listed in a notebook the thirty-nine bird species he had seen. "I like wrens," he wrote, "because they do more good than almost any other bird, they sing sweetly, they are very pretty, and very tame." Aldo would aim his slingshot at the crows and English house sparrows that pestered his songbirds.

The best time of the year for Aldo came in August. That's when the Leopolds and Starkers traveled to an island resort on Lake Huron called Les Cheneaux. Marquette Island, alive with wild areas, was ideal for exploring. Woods covered the land, and there were no roads. Walking trails connected the clubhouse, tennis courts, and golf course. Groceries were towed out by boat.

Aldo tramped over the island paths, making maps of the hills and plants. His eyes scanned the woods for birds and animal signs. Often he, his father, and Carl Jr. would camp out for three or four days, fishing and foraging. The "men" made it their challenge to live off the land. Blueberries and beach plums spiced up their morning pancakes. A touch of squirrel meat or trout added zest to their rice-and-potato stews.

The Les Cheneaux trip always ended too quickly. But once they were back in Iowa, it was hunting time. On Saturdays, Aldo's father woke him long before sunup for a big breakfast. Calling their dogs, the two walked down to the train station. It was a quick trip to one of the hunting clubs on the Illinois side of the river. By sunrise they were perched atop a muskrat mound, squatting in the mud, waiting for ducks.

Spud and seven-year-old Aldo show off his catch at the cabin at Les Cheneaux.

Since there were few hunting laws in the late 1800s, hunters baited hungry birds with corn. Then they shot the huge flocks that swept in. Birds of all kinds, from eagles to pigeons, were killed by the wagonload. Aldo's father bristled over these unsportsmanlike actions. He set his own rules and limits. Carl never hunted in the spring, when the number of birds was the lowest, and he didn't use bait. He always followed wounded animals to put them out of pain. He never shot for trophies, and he stopped hunting rare animals altogether. Wild game was a big treat in the Leopold and Starker households, yet Carl never brought home more than the family could eat in a week.

Carl passed on his hunting rules to his children. For many years, Carl made Aldo carry a stick that had been carved to look and feel like a gun. Aldo had to prove he could tote the stick all day without getting careless. Then, around the age of eleven, he was awarded a single-shot shotgun. He learned to make each shot count. "Never point a gun at anything you don't intend to kill" was Carl's stern law. Aldo, like his brothers, became a crackerjack marksman.

As the seasons changed, so did Aldo's activities. Just after his thirteenth birthday, though, Aldo's life shifted painfully. Opa and Oma died a few months apart. His family moved into the Big House, filling the empty spaces, and Aldo entered high school.

Burlington High School was overcrowded, and Aldo was too shy to stand out. Observing everyone with his serious blue-green eyes, he said little. He

Aldo's father, Carl Leopold, is dressed for the hunt with his dog, Flick, around 1900, when Aldo was about thirteen.

preferred to escape by streetcar to Flint Creek to watch kingfishers and crayfish. Although the school was known for its difficulty, Aldo rose to the top of his class (except in math). English, history, and biology suited him best. He devoured stories of sportsmen and adventurers, explorers and scientists. Seeing his promise, his English teacher encouraged and challenged him. He collected favorite quotations and kept journals of his observations of nature.

Clara doted on her eldest child. Though she loved the outdoors as well, she didn't want all the time he spent outside to roughen him. So she pressed him into reading novels, poetry, plays, and philosophy (which he liked). She even forced him into dance lessons (which he didn't like). But nothing could take the outdoors out of Aldo.

This early notebook sketch by Aldo captures of one of his beloved backyard birds, the house wren.

The Leopold Desks

BUILT ON HONOR
TO ENDURE.

BY THE

RAND & LEOPOLD DESK CO.

BURLINGTON, IOWA,
U. S. A.

This advertisement for Aldo's father's company showed the family emphasis on values, honor, and ethics that Aldo carried with him into all aspects of life.

Since his father ran the Leopold Desk Company and it depended on wood, Aldo paid attention to the lumber industry. The nation's forests were being cut faster than they could grow back. In the 1890s, while Aldo was growing up, the United States had begun to set aside forest reserves to protect the trees. Then, while Aldo was in high school, one of the country's first forestry schools opened at Yale University. Aldo knew immediately what he wanted to do. If he could become a forester, he could get paid to work in the woods all day. How could a job get any better?

# 2
# To Be a Forester

At sixteen, Aldo said good-bye to Burlington High. He was heading out East in January to a high-class boarding school. He figured if he could do well there, he ought to have a chance at Yale University. Before he went, though, he wanted one last shot at adventure.

The Leopolds skipped Les Cheneaux that summer and loaded up their canvas tents for Estes Park, Colorado. When August came to a close, Aldo and his father split off from the family to travel northwest for an expedition through the wilds of Yellowstone National Park. Later they joined two other fathers and sons for a big-game hunting trip in Montana.

On the trail, there was excitement around every turn. Geysers spewed steam, and rivers rushed through colored stone canyons. A bear stampeded their horses and later raided their supply wagon, leaving behind a trail of half-eaten sausages. Afterward, a blizzard locked them in camp. No one shot much. By trip's end, though, Aldo had added forty new bird species to his list.

Upon his return home, Aldo had to get ready for school. Lawrenceville Preparatory School was

Aldo, "the Shark" and "the Naturalist," looks like a serious
student in his Lawrenceville Academy photo.

several hundred miles away, amid New Jersey pas-
turelands, marshes, and wooded ridges. Aldo arrived
there by train on January 6, 1904, five days before
his seventeenth birthday. Within two days, he was
tramping about the countryside.

The move wasn't easy. It was Aldo's first time
away from his family, and he didn't fit in at Lawrenceville. His midwestern accent sounded strange
to his eastern and southern classmates, and he was a
year and a half behind them.

Lawrenceville impressed Aldo as it was built like a prestigious
East Coast university with large stone buildings edging a common green. This is Upper House, which sat along with other
resident houses, the chapel, and classroom buildings.

Aldo, however, was unusual enough to be interesting. His classmates nicknamed him the Naturalist

and teased him constantly. Aldo held himself proudly aloof. He saw himself as more studious than the rest. Soon, though, some of the fellows were asking to go with him on his hikes. They thought it would be good for some laughs, but they got caught up in the explorations too. And Aldo found they weren't such bad fellows after all.

While Aldo was away at Lawrenceville, his mother waited daily for the mail. He'd write pages and pages, detailing the discoveries he'd made on his woodland tramps. He penned so many letters home that writing became a lifelong habit. Few things escaped his notice. Aldo knew the habits of some birds so well that he worried when they didn't arrive back from migration at their usual time. On April 13, 1904, he wrote home:

> There I was, walking along and just thinking of the overdue birds, when far away up the stream I heard the rattle of a kingfisher...I made a record going up the bank of that creek. And when I arrived, sure enough, he was there, rattling and plunging in true kingfisher fashion. It would be putting it tamely to say I felt relieved.

Migrating birds were on his father's mind too. Carl was back in Iowa, pushing for state laws to

Home for a break from Lawrenceville, Aldo displays his hunting gear and dog in his backyard, next to the greenhouse.

protect the birds—especially the ducks and other game birds. But other hunters were fighting against him. Aldo wrote to his father, trying to cheer him:

I am very sorry that the ducks are being slaugh-
tered as usual, but of course could expect nothing
else. When my turn comes to have something to
say and do against it..., I am sure nothing in my
power will be lacking to the good cause.

Until then, Aldo put his time to good use.
From the library he checked out Charles Darwin's book
*A Naturalist's Voyage Round the World.* He found it
"very instructive and interesting." Also intriguing was
a lecture by a Dakota Sioux Indian named Ohiyesa–
Charles Alexander Eastman. Aldo was so impressed by
his talk that he wrote home to his mother:

> Like a true Indian, he talks little, says a great
> deal to those who have understanding and noth-
> ing to those who have not...Some words and
> phrases which I have never heard anywhere else
> impressed me particularly. He said, after speak-
> ing of the Indian's knowledge of nature, "Nature
> is the gate to the Great Mystery." The words are
> simple enough, but the meaning unfathomable.

Aldo puzzled on these mysteries of life and
God and nature but came to no conclusions. His
hours were filled with the woods, playing baseball,

swimming, running track, skipping class occasionally (when he could afford to), and a lot of studying. Aldo did so well in his courses that the fellows called him "the Shark." (But mathematics still got the best of him.) Aldo caught up to his classmates and graduated with them. He sailed through Yale's entrance exams and was on his way.

The forestry program at Yale was for graduate students only, so in September 1905 Aldo enrolled in Yale's Sheffield Scientific School to earn his college degree. He moved into a room at 400 Temple Street and set to the arduous task of studying physics, chemistry, mechanical drawing, and geometry. All at once, he had little time for bird-watching and plant collecting. He slid into a new world of dances, football games, yachting, fraternities, and parties. He changed from a penny-pincher who liked his old field clothes to what his brother Frederick called "a dude." Soon Aldo stood out on campus as the man with the striped tailored suits and jazzy ties. "He didn't think he was cut from the common cloth," said Frederick, "and he wasn't."

Though Aldo had discovered a taste for fancy clothes and high-class doings, he hadn't completely ended his outdoor explorations. Aldo befriended a boy named Bennie Jacobosky whose parents had little

Aldo, now a snappy dresser in a bowtie, enjoys boating and tennis at Les Cheneaux with friends and his sister, Marie (back, to his left).

money and little time for their son. Aldo showed Bennie the woods, and Bennie showed Aldo how people who were less fortunate often lived. Aldo started to see himself as someone who had "received everything and done little."

To make up for his good fortune, Aldo drove himself hard, trying to prove his worth. In his third year at Sheffield, his discipline cracked. He discovered that college women were far more interesting than college courses. Aldo cut classes and stopped studying. Eventually the college dean threatened to kick him out of school. His parents threatened to cut the purse strings.

Aldo got the message. He quit going to dances. He quit attending football games. His only time outdoors was put to chopping, thinning, surveying, and mapping trees. He passed his final exams and received a bachelor's degree in June 1908. The next fall, he officially entered the Yale Forestry School for a one-year master's degree program.

The end was finally in sight. He joined the Society of Robin Hood and let Yale form him into the perfect forest ranger.

# 3

# Leather Chaps and a Ten-Gallon Hat

By the time Aldo graduated from the Yale Forestry School in 1909, the United States Forest Service (USFS) managed over 150 million wooded acres. Gifford Pinchot, the director of the USFS, looked at the forests like a bank account. They made money for the country–trees were sold for chopping timber and permits were sold for grazing livestock. A forest ranger's job was to manage these sales and protect the forests from fire and disease. A healthy crop of trees had to be saved in the national account.

The Forest Service hired Aldo shortly after his graduation, and he was sent off to the wilds of District 3–to the Apache National Forest, in Arizona Territory. This forest had only been protected as a national reserve for one year. The area had been taken from the Apache, and the lands were still wild.

No roads crossed the Apache National Forest. One could only get there by stagecoach and horse. Leather chaps and a ten-gallon hat were necessities. Aldo spent his first paycheck on them, as well as on

Aldo and his dog Flip rest on a stump at an old mine in the
Apache National Forest in 1910.

blue jeans and a bandanna, a pair of revolvers, a saddle, and a horse. He picked Jiminy Hicks for his steed.
After a few weeks, Aldo purchased another essen-
tial–a rubber butt plate to soften that saddle a bit.

Aldo swaggered around the forest lands, climb-
ing mountains and flicking fishing lines into rushing
streams. In an adobe bunkhouse, he lived with the
other bachelor foresters. Together the men fought
fires, made deals with loggers, played sandlot baseball,
and lived the cowboy life. But he also had to calcu-
late timber sales, plant seeds for spruce trees, and
inspect lumber mills.

A month after arriving, Aldo received his first big assignment. He took over the leadership of a crew that was mapping the landscape and trees for timber on the Apache's Blue Mountains. Each cruiser was sent out alone for a day or two to survey and map out three square miles. Their tools were a compass, pace counter, barometer, and notebook. For Aldo, the mapping brought him back to the joys of his youth but the pacing and math calculations did not. Not only did he have to do his own cruising, but he also had to check the other cruisers' work, scout out places for their camps, and oversee those cooking and handling supplies.

This group of timber cruisers, as they were called, were old hands and didn't appreciate their new camp leader–he stuck out as a cocky tenderfoot from the first. He got lost more than once. He acted as if he knew everything and miscalculated surveys. Worse yet, he didn't bring enough food and he made the men cook over open fires and eat deer instead of beef.

He even abandoned his work at times to go hunting (for that deer meat) or chase after illegal hunters. The Apache, naturally, thought they could still hunt on their lands, but the rangers wanted to stop them, especially Aldo. He wanted to protect the game from any overhunting (of course, he didn't consider *his* hunting a threat!), and he was pondering a side project. Would the Forest Service consider setting up a game refuge in the Blue Mountains? Many large game animals, such as deer, elk, and bighorn sheep, were becoming scarce, and Aldo and the other foresters wanted to protect their numbers. His boss had given him permission to map out his plan and the area.

The rangers also saw it as their job to shoot mountain lions, wolves, and grizzly bears. They figured the more predators they killed, the safer the cattle and sheep would be—and the more game there'd be. While out on the Blue with another ranger, Aldo spotted a mother wolf with cubs. Full of hunters' zeal, they

Aldo (far left) and his reconnaissance team of 1910 timber cruisers bury their biscuits in protest to the cook and call the place Camp Indigestion.

blasted her. Aldo's aim was right on, but his heart wasn't. The wolf's gaze struck him with a dead-on *Why?* He was left with no sure answer. As he moved in closer to check his shot, the dying wolf snatched his rifle butt in her teeth. Aldo jumped back but would never forget the "fierce green fire" in her eyes.

Despite the uncertainties and rough spots, Aldo loved the forester's life. He wrote home to his father urging him to come out to the Blue Mountains:

> Now you and the Kid come out here, get you a
> small dog and a couple of horses and just snoop
> around here for a month. I'll bet you can land
> some fine hides and some very succulent trout.

When the cruisers returned, late and over budget, Aldo was in hot water. His supervisor, Arthur Ringland, heard a long list of complaints. Arthur called for an investigation. Cocky and conceited, Aldo welcomed it. He thought for sure it would clear his name.

The investigation only smirched it more. The possibility of being fired hung over his head. Fortunately for Aldo, Arthur decided his mistakes grew out of inexperience. He had Aldo fix all his errors that winter and hand in a clean report. He would give Aldo one more chance.

That chance came the next summer. Aldo led a new team of timber cruisers, and this time the members were more inexperienced than he was. And he had learned from his mistakes. He measured more carefully, guided his group more efficiently, laughed more often, listened to others' advice, and carried a humbler opinion of himself. This time his crew did well on all counts, and Aldo wrote home that it was "the best summer I have ever had."

In March 1911, Arthur called Aldo to work at the district's headquarters, in Albuquerque. He wanted to get to know better how this new ranger could handle management work before deciding his next post.

Twenty-four-year-old Aldo loved the excitement of being back in a town again—the dances, theater, circus, parties, and Wild West shows. He was loafing about in an Albuquerque drugstore with Ringland when Anita and Estella Bergere walked in, two beauties from a well-to-do ranching family. Arthur introduced Aldo to the sisters, and within the week the two foresters were invited to a party at the Bergere home in Santa Fe. Both men gladly accepted.

The night they arrived, the ranch was all lit up with paper lanterns. Young women in colorful dresses wove in and out of the crowds with small bird-shaped

Aldo joins the rest of the Apache National Foresters at the Albuquerque headquarters. He is smoking a pipe on the front steps (center right).

lamps. Like an exotic bird herself, twenty-one-year-old Estella glided to Aldo and handed him her parrot. This was clearly an invitation to dance. Aldo smiled and took her hand.

The schoolteacher had a gentle, laughing way about her. No one is sure what Aldo said to Arthur after that dance, but "Ring" got the message. He assigned Aldo to the Carson National Forest—the closest forest to Santa Fe and the dark-haired, kind-eyed Estella Bergere.

# 4
# Matters of Life and Death

Aldo returned to the Apache to pack his gear and sell his horse. On the way to his new post, he stopped in Santa Fe. Afterward he wrote to his sister, "Estella is a wonder on a horse, and...she is very much of a peach."

Aldo shows off his new horse, Polly, at his new post in the Carson National Forest.

Aldo, though, had one big concern. Estella was seeing someone else in Santa Fe while Aldo would be stationed a whole day's train ride away. The best he could do was woo her by mail. Which he did, with long, descriptive letters. In his first letter, he told her about his new horse, Polly, who was a beauty:

> Don't you love a horse with a soft gray nose? I'm
> sure you would love Polly if you could see his long
> graceful gliding trot and the pretty arch in his neck–
> and the soft gray nose would clinch the argument.

Aldo railroaded on to the Carson in May 1911. He was stricken with disappointment. This forest was far tamer than the Apache. Too many sheep and cattle had grazed the Carson's lands. Aldo wrote, "There is practically no game in this country. Of course the sheep have run out all the deer."

Aldo and his new boss, Harry C. Hall, had been hired to stop the overgrazing. They were to grant fewer grazing permits and promptly arrest offenders. They slung pistols from their hips to show the ranchers and herders they meant business.

But it was Aldo's pen that became his most force-ful tool. He started a newsletter for rangers called the *Carson Pine Cone*. Aldo used it to "scatter seeds of

Aldo takes Estella for a walk on the railroad tracks (with her brother Joe, it seems), trying to win her heart and steal her from her other boyfriend.

knowledge, encouragement, and enthusiasm." Most of the *Pine Cone*'s articles, poems, jokes, editorials, and drawings were Aldo's own. His readers soon realized that the forest animals were as important to him as the trees. His goal was to bring back the "flavor of the wilds."

And to capture Estella's heart. He visited whenever he could. One night he wrote to her:

> The night is so wonderful that it almost hurts.
> I wonder if you are seeing the myriad of little
> "Scharfches wolken" I told you about—do you
> remember the "little sheep clouds"? I have never

seen them so perfect as they are tonight. I would
like to be out in *our canyon*...and see that wild
Clematis in the moonlight–wouldn't you?

In the fall, Ring paid Aldo an unexpected visit at
Carson to bring him news: Estella's beau had proposed.
Now love letters weren't enough. Aldo made a mad
dash to offer his own passionate marriage proposal.

Estella was overcome. She needed time to
think. She'd only known him four months. For almost
three more months, letters passed back and forth.

Aldo and Estella are thrilled on their wedding day, October 9,
1912, accompanied by Aldo's brother Carl and Estella's sister
Dolores. They later wed too.

Aldo had trouble concentrating. Finally, he shuttled to Santa Fe for an answer.

Yes, said Estella, YES. Her father only said maybe, but Estella said no one could change her mind. Aldo was so thrilled he could think of nothing to say when he wrote home.

A few months after his engagement, twenty-five-year-old Aldo was promoted to acting supervisor. He was busier than ever, working with the cowmen and sheepers. In his free time, he built a home looking over the Rio Grande Valley for his bride-to-be. Aldo brought her back to the little house after their wedding, in October 1912. Estella learned to hunt, skin, and cook with Aldo at her side. In the evenings, the newlyweds laughed and read to each other by the firelight. Aldo was "very grateful to just be."

The Leopolds discovered in the spring that they were expecting a child. Estella decided to visit her family while Aldo attended to sheep business in a distant section of the forest. He rode from one lambing area to the next, camping under the stars.

Unfortunately, the stars were not out most of those April evenings. A storm hit. It sleeted, snowed, hailed, and rained for two days. Aldo slept outside those nights curled up in a soaked, icy bedroll. He decided to take a shortcut and lost his way in the black of night. An Apache man found him wandering aimlessly in the cold. He brought Aldo to his home, offering him food and a warm place to sleep. Shivering, Aldo climbed on his horse and rode toward the nearest railway tracks to flag down a train.

As he rode, Aldo's legs swelled so much he had to slash his boots open. Eventually he straggled by stage coach into Chama, New Mexico. There a doctor gave him medicine for swollen joints. Aldo thought he would recover.

But he didn't. By the time he arrived back at Carson headquarters, he was so swollen he could hardly move. His assistant, Ray Marsh, insisted he see a doctor in Santa Fe. If Aldo had not taken his advice, he would likely have died within the week. His kidneys had failed. Deadly poisons were building up in his blood and muscles.

The doctor sent him to bed immediately. Estella and the Bergeres piled blankets on him and gave him sweating pills. Slowly, Aldo's body rid itself of the poisons, and his kidneys began cleaning his blood once again.

His healing, though, only inched forward. Aldo remained in bed for six weeks, losing weight. His body failed to gain strength. Ray Marsh took over Aldo's duties at the Carson.

On June 6, 1913, Estella, large with their child, and Aldo, broken and weak, boarded a train for Burlington, Iowa. Doted upon once more by his mother and family, Aldo could do little more than sit on the Leopold porch with his pipe and a book. He watched the birds and thought about his life. He still had not done what he had promised he'd do—protect wild birds and game animals. Up to now, he had had big plans, but no time. Now all he had was time.

So he wrote articles for the *Pine Cone*, urging his fellow foresters to work for the health of the whole forest. He proposed that the forest animals could and should be managed just like the trees. In the fall, big news blazed in the *Pine Cone*. On October 22, 1913, Estella gave birth to a boy: Aldo Starker Leopold. No one could have been prouder than the baby's father. He wrote to one of his Yale professors, "A brand new Forest Supervisor arrived here."

Aldo and Estella traveled back to New Mexico to show off their son to Estella's family, the Bergeres. A full year after his illness, Aldo was still weak. His final leave of absence from the Forest Service ran out in May 1914. He was officially out of a job. Now he and his family had to live off the generosity of the Leopolds and Bergeres. Aldo felt helpless.

In June, his doctor called him back from New

As he works to recover, Aldo fishes at the Rio Grande.

Things Natural, Wild, and Free

Mexico to Burlington. Carl Sr. had had surgery, and the two of them could recover together. Which they did. But Aldo's spirits were low and dipping lower.

Arthur Ringland wanted Aldo back in the Forest Service as badly as Aldo wanted to return. A letter arrived in Burlington from Ring describing a desk job in the district's grazing office. Aldo snatched the opportunity. It wasn't the job he wanted, but it was a job.

Aldo, Estella, and one-year-old Starker moved into a small bungalow on 14th Street in Albuquerque. When home from work, Aldo played with the ever-moving Starker, built wooden toys and decoys, gardened, and studied Spanish with Estella. He tried to forget the endless paperwork at his job. In November, he wrote to his father:

> Neither you nor I have worried the ducks much
> lately, have we?...I wish I could be on hand so we
> could *talk* ducks, anyhow, but so goes it.

Then one night in December 1914, a startling telegram arrived. Carl Leopold Sr. had died.

Aldo knew he could wait no longer to act. He had promised his father he would do something for the wild creatures they both loved. The time had come.

# 5

# There's More to a Forest Than Trees

Less than a month after his father's death and a few days before his twenty-eighth birthday, Aldo Leopold handed in a memo to his supervisors. It outlined ways to increase the number of game animals in the forests. His plan was noted and passed on to Washington, DC. Not a single policy changed.

More than ever, Aldo wanted out of his job. But where was he to go? Arthur Ringland came to the rescue again. He designed a job just for Aldo—he would develop programs and guidelines for game protection, publicity, and public recreation for the forests of District 3. Aldo wrote to his mother:

> I don't trust this new job to last, much less like it. However, I'm so...glad to be making a living that I gladly waive the fine questions.

In some ways, Aldo was pleasantly surprised as the job took him to one of the country's natural treasures: the Grand Canyon. On June 15, 1915, he

This is part of the beauty that Aldo was trying to preserve:
the stretch of the Colorado River just before the Sockdolager
Rapids in the Grand Canyon.

peered down the canyon and around its edges. Billboards and electric lights dotted the rim. Shopkeepers with megaphones barked at tourists on horses and in Model Ts. Garbage piled up everywhere, and sewage drained into the river. The destruction was appalling.

The canyon was both a national monument and a game refuge. Aldo needed to find ways for the tourists and hunters to be able to enjoy the canyon without spoiling it. Over the next two years, he worked with the forest's supervisor, Don P. Johnston, on the first complete recreation and preservation plan for the Grand Canyon. They developed more effective campgrounds, trails, sewage systems, and rules for recreation and businesses.

After his canyon survey, Aldo plotted out areas in District 3 for bird sanctuaries and wildlife refuges. He then wrote a wildlife management handbook for rangers. It laid out new hunting and fishing laws, described species, and explained methods for stocking animals and fish in the Southwest. This handy manual, the *Game and Fish Handbook*, was the first of its kind for the Forest Service. It gained such praise that the national office finally paid attention. It even passed it on to other forest districts as a model.

In October 1915, shortly after the handbook's publication, Aldo's second son, Luna Bergere Leopold, was born. In the months to follow, Aldo launched part three of his game-protection strategy. He sent out a flock of letters to local sportsmen asking them to work together for the protection of game animals. Soon Aldo was trekking through New Mexico and Arizona, organizing game-protection clubs.

With quiet charm, enthusiasm, and logic, Aldo convinced sportsmen that they would have nothing to hunt if they did not work to save the remaining wild animals. Small conservation groups sprang up, and in March 1916, the New Mexico Game Protective Association was formed. The members dedicated themselves to killing off predators, enforcing stricter hunting laws, and setting aside areas where game animals would be totally protected. Aldo became the group's secretary. Resurrecting an old title, Aldo produced a newsletter for interested foresters and hunters. The goal of the new *Pine Cone* was "to promote the protection and enjoyment of wild things." By that summer, Aldo felt well enough to do a little hunting again.

In January 1917, near his thirtieth birthday, Aldo received a letter of congratulations from former president Theodore Roosevelt: "My dear Mr. Leopold,...I think your platform simply capital...Your association in New Mexico is setting an example to the whole country." Buoyed, Aldo ramped up his

**THE PINE CONE**

APRIL 1916 — ISSUED QUARTERLY

OFFICIAL BULLETIN OF THE NEW MEXICO GAME PROTECTIVE ASSOCIATION

The April 1916 issue of *The Pine Cone* lays out the association's commitment to game laws and "a vigorous campaign against predatory animals."

efforts "to restore to every citizen his inalienable right to know and love the wild things of his native land."

While game-protection societies were springing up across the Southwest and the nation, war was exploding across Europe. Then in April 1917, the United States entered the fight to support the European allies against Germany. The nation thrust aside conservation efforts. Forests were sliced up to make biplanes. Cattle slated for army rations overgrazed the plains and the forest slopes. Foresters became soldiers.

Because of his ill health, Aldo was not drafted. He was promoted. The recommendation stated: "Mr. Leopold is a very brilliant man and an accomplished all around Forest officer. He is considered one of the brainiest men in the District."

There's More to a Forest Than Trees   45

In August, the Leopolds also celebrated the birth of their first daughter: Adelina, nicknamed Nina. Money was in short supply, and Aldo was discouraged by the ravaging of the forests, Forest Service staff, and game-protection efforts while the war raged on. So when the Albuquerque Chamber of Commerce offered him a job at a higher salary, he took it, in January 1918.

For the next year and a half, Leopold advertised the advantages of Albuquerque and its businesses, speaking to citizen and business groups and sportsmen. He pressed the chamber to create more parks, build traditional Hispanic architecture, and hire a city planner. He also proposed a park along the city's banks of the Rio Grande.

The war treaty was signed in November 1918, and just after the new year, Theodore Roosevelt died. Yet in February, Roosevelt's dream of creating a national park at the Grand Canyon was realized. The plan Aldo helped develop was enhanced and modified to permanently preserve the canyon.

With the war over and much work to be done, the Forest Service wanted Aldo back as much as he wanted to return. So in August 1919, he assumed the position of second in command of Forest District 3. It was his duty to inspect the daily operations of its forests. He had to check that they were running

properly on every level, making recommendations
for improvements.

Aldo's first reports were so sketchy and vague
they were of little concrete use. His supervisor won-
dered if he was suited to the task. So he sent a hard-
core army officer, Evan Kelley, to evaluate Aldo and
show him the ropes.

Kelley drilled him into developing a thorough
eye for detail in the land and operations. He described
Aldo's drastic awakening, "Highbrow ideas have been
blasted by seeing affairs in their true aspects." Aldo
soon took such organized and specific notes on everything from logbooks to outhouses that his reports drasti-
cally multiplied in weight. Few things escaped his notice.

Always ready to go out into the field for an adventure, Estella
did it with style. Here she is on their porch steps with Luna,
Starker, and Nina (left to right) in 1919.

Aldo examined the southwestern forests so closely that he began to notice the hillsides and riverbanks scarred by ravines. Cattle and sheep had eaten and ground away the cover of grasses. The loose soil had been swept by wind and driven by rain into rivers, muddying them up. The blanket of dirt was smothering the fish, and the sun was baking the leftover soil into brick. The land was shifting to desert. Aldo put the soil on his list of concerns.

For a break, Aldo took a camping trip to an area in Mexico where the Colorado River flowed into the Gulf of California. There in the delta, Aldo discovered a place where wildlife and plants flourished like paradise. The soil had not been overgrazed or washed away. These lush, healthy wildlands clearly outshone the forests of his district. Yet years ago, both lands had started out very much alike.

*There must be ways to stop the soil from being worn away*, Aldo thought. Erosion control soared to the top of his action list. He began researching the topic of protecting watersheds–rivers, streams, and lakes–from dirt washing into them. He gathered evidence from each forest in the district. This turned into a bigger project than he expected: the Forest Service's first *Watershed Handbook*. This manual told foresters how to protect rivers and lakes by preventing soil erosion.

Each passing year had made Aldo see the forest as something more than just trees. There were the wild animals, grasses and wildflowers, soil, rivers, and lakes. He had made progress on protecting all of them. He had galvanized hunters in the Southwest into protecting game and creating game-protection societies. He had made the whole Forest Service more aware of soil conservation, and he had even begun to think fires had an important natural role in keeping forests healthy.

Now he envisioned still another quality of forests that needed protection—wildness itself. The wild lands in Mexico had showed him that. Throughout the country, places that were rare and spectacular were being ruined by human "improvements." Aldo began to wonder if the best use of these wild areas was no modern use at all. No roads. No grazing. No logging. No mining. No tourist cabins.

This was a shocking idea. Most people wanted to put every piece of land to some definable use. Aldo teamed up with another forester, Arthur Carhart, to push for the protection of two specific wild places: the Gila Canyon area in New Mexico and Trappers Lake in Colorado. "It will be much easier to keep wilderness areas," Aldo noted, "than to create them." In fact, he observed, the last option "may be dismissed as impossible." From this point on, Aldo set out to

It's a windy day at the Boundary Waters Area of Minnesota and Canada during Aldo's first canoe-camping visit, so they jury-rig a sail with crossed paddles and a jacket.

change a nation's mind about what its remaining patches of wilderness were for. He delivered speeches and wrote articles about the "wilderness idea." Wild places could not be grown like timber, he argued. They could only be saved from destruction.

At thirty-seven, with four children (Aldo Carl was born in 1919), Aldo was respected nationally, and now even internationally. The Forest Service loved his "splendid imagination," his hard work and ability to learn new things quickly, his passion for scientific exploration, and his "enormous range of interests and knowledge." So the service shifted him out of field work and assigned him to the job of assistant director of the Forest Products Laboratory, in Madison, Wisconsin. His supervisors hinted that he would soon be promoted to director.

Perhaps Aldo felt he had accomplished all he could in a field position. Or maybe he was looking for a promotion to a director or the scientific challenges a laboratory could offer. He might even have been pressured into taking the job. But his days as a forester ended. He accepted the job.

Before it started, he, his brothers, and Starker escaped on a canoe camping trip to the wilderness waters between Minnesota and Ontario, Canada. These loon-dotted lakes and rivers were filled with fish and edged by pines and granite outcroppings. These northern lands had a completely different feel from the wilderness areas of the Southwest and Mexico. But they were just as beautiful and exciting. Aldo wrote in his trip journal, "It has been a memorable trip, maybe the best we ever made...How Dad would have loved it!"

On June 3, 1924, five days after Aldo left the Southwest, one of his biggest triumphs occurred—the Forest Service approved of his plan for the Gila Wilderness Area. This was the first wild place to be so protected by the US Forest Service. For this reason, Aldo Leopold earned the title "father of the national wilderness system."

# 6

# Starting a Science

The sun glinted off Lake Wingra. Boys with fishing poles and stringers of sunfish dotted the shore. *The children will like Madison*, Aldo thought. *But Estella won't.* No more warm winters, adobe homes, red-tiled roofs, chickens in the yard, or Spanish on the tongue. Instead, it would be months of freezing and snow, redbrick and painted wooden homes with neat, green lawns, and everything in English. Estella would cry many times in those early months.

But even Estella cheered up when the family bought a stucco home on Van Hise Avenue in Madison. Aldo led the family in a 1924 spring planting of trees, bushes, and wildflowers. They hung birdhouses and feeders, and explored the city's lakes.

At the laboratory, the acidic odors of wood glues and varnishes bit the stale air. It was hardly the place for Aldo. He preferred a live tree in the forest to a tin of shavings in an experiment. But for the next four years, he directed lab research on wood products. He helped discover new uses for the otherwise wasted parts of trees and lumber.

However, the best part of his day began in

Aldo looks like the professional in his official portrait as the assistant director of the United States Forest Products Laboratory, where he felt "like a fish out of water."

the evening. He and Estella would listen to classical music, and Aldo would quiz his four rowdy, quick-brained kids about the interesting things they had done and learned during the day. As a family, they took up the art and sport of archery. On winter evenings, Aldo would go down to his basement workshop. There, he carved, sanded, glued, and balanced his own bows and arrows for hunting. He taught the rest of the family to make their own archery gear too.

Aldo, Carl, and either Luna or Starker are practicing archery, often roving and choosing different targets as they move.

Sundays, the Leopolds often packed up their gear for a picnic in Wingra Park. They roved the grounds, choosing targets for their arrows. (Estella became so skilled that she won archery tournaments and taught classes in archery at the university.)

Family campouts and hunting trips were highlights for all. About once a year, Aldo and his brothers got together for a weeklong canoe trip. And in 1927, a final member joined the family, little Estella. She too grew up surrounded by the smells of oak smoke from campfires and damp leaves in the woods.

Aldo had never stopped working to protect game animals and preserve the wilderness. He was a national leader in the American Game Association as well as other national scientific organizations. He had joined several conservation groups in Wisconsin. But Aldo could live off of these passions for only so long. He needed work that meant something to him.

The Sporting Arms and Ammunition Manufacturers' Institute approached him with an unusual job offer. This group of gun and bullet makers wanted to make sure the sport of hunting didn't die out. So they asked Aldo to examine American conservation methods to see which ones worked best for game animals. It was a risky proposal. No one had ever tried such a project before, and if the institute didn't like his findings or methods, it would be free to fire him after a year.

Despite the risk, forty-one-year-old Aldo accepted the job. He told Estella, "I must have an instinct for poker." In July 1928, he set out for Minnesota and later Michigan. For a few weeks or more, he rattled through each state in his beat-up Ford. He interviewed lawmakers, foresters, farmers, business-people, and hunters, making detailed reports as he had done in the Forest Service. As he examined the midwestern states, he saw a trend. Wherever there was "clean" farming, a method in which grass was plowed or eaten by livestock down to the soil, few wild birds and other animals thrived. But wherever farmers left grasses near fences, woods, and swamps for cover and food, wildlife was plentiful.

Aldo returned to Madison between trips. The University of Wisconsin had lent him a small office, and he had hired a part-time secretary. Every time he came back, he piled mounds of notes, letters, and reports on her desk to be typed. "I was astounded at the amount of data he could collect," she said, "and how steadily he could work assembling the data and turning out reports after his return." She boasted to her friends about her great job: "He was the kind of boss who complimented me when I did well, and passed over my mistakes or overlooked them alto-gether. No wonder I grew devoted to him." The work piles rose as he also polished the first chapters of a book—*Deer Management in the Southwest*.

As the 1920s came to an end, a time of hard-ship hit, known as the Great Depression. Banks and businesses across the country closed. Many farmers lost their land. Thousands of people were out of jobs and broke. Conservation efforts were again shoved aside.

Aldo's *Report on a Game Survey of the North Central States* was published in 1931. It was the most in-depth summary of the state of American wildlife the nation had ever seen. Instantly he became the expert in the new field of game conservation and management. He also had begun to change his mind about predators. They were not the enemies of wildlife, loss of habitat was.

The survey had answered questions about the Midwest, but funds to survey other areas ran low. Aldo knew he would need a new job soon. He decided to scrap the *Deer Management* project. He assembled the scientific information he had gathered into a textbook, *Game Management*, which could be used to teach the new science.

To test some of his management methods, Aldo formed the Riley Game Cooperative. He convinced a group of hunters and farmers to improve the farmers' lands for wildlife. The farmers agreed to leave brush piles, grasses, and trees on the edges of their fields and to plant plots of crops for grouse, quail, and pheasants. The hunters chipped in money and hard work.

Aldo and Flick try out the hunting on the Riley Game Preserve that he created through a cooperative partnership of farmers and hunters.

The experiment succeeded. No longer did the farmers have trouble with trespassing hunters. The hunters had a great place to hunt, and the farmers made extra money. Even better, more wild birds lived in the area than had lived there in years.

In July 1931, Aldo attended a scientific conference on plant and animal population cycles in Canada. He met some of the world's greatest minds in biology and ecology. This new science studied the relationships between living things and their natural surroundings. Now Aldo was pondering how the cycles of plants, animals, fish, insects, diseases, and weather affect each other. His focus shifted from saving game animals and songbirds to saving all animals. He wanted to study all the interconnected cogs and wheels in nature's system.

Less than a year later, in 1932, the funding for Aldo's game-management work was slashed. He was on his own in the midst of the Depression. A publishing company agreed to publish *Game Management* if he could finish it quickly and help pay the costs. It was another big risk. But Aldo pulled five hundred dollars from his savings and went to work full time on the book.

Estella probably felt the money worries most since she had to make ends meet. For the next year and a half, the family scraped by on savings, money from Leopold stocks, and possibly small gifts from their relatives in Iowa and New Mexico.

Aldo received job offers at distant locations; he refused them. He didn't want to move the family or

Without Estella to make his life work smoothly, Aldo couldn't have been who he was. They loved being with each other, and she enjoyed the outdoors as much as he did.

quit working on the book. He was too close to finishing. The book was dedicated to his father, "a pioneer in sportsmanship." He completed it in July 1932.

All the while, Aldo aimed for a position at the University of Wisconsin. He wanted to do field research and train game-management professionals. But the university lacked funds, so Aldo set himself up as a consulting forester. Conservation organizations hired him to inspire their members and the public.

The Civilian Conservation Corps was a great government program that got many of the nation's unemployed young men outdoors, doing needed work, and getting paid.

Landowners and states asked him how to manage their lands for the best use for humans *and* wildlife

The United States was one of his clients. They had him direct soil-conservation efforts in the South-west with the Civilian Conservation Corps. These groups of young unmarried men, from eighteen to twenty-five, worked at replanting trees and building walls, trails, campgrounds, parks, and fire towers, among other tasks. For many city boys, it was their first taste of the outdoor life, and many, like Aldo, fell in love with it.

# 7
# Ecology in Practice

Published in the spring of 1933, *Game Management* was selling well by summer. It had been praised by scientists and conservationists alike. *American Forests* magazine said that it "will stand not only as the book of the year, but the book of the decade in game conservation." In August, the University of Wisconsin announced that it was launching a graduate program in game management. And they had hired the most qualified person in the country to direct it–Aldo Leopold. He became the nation's first professor in the new field.

The university expected Aldo to do more than just teach game management, however. It wanted him to teach all the citizens of Wisconsin how to put conservation into practice.

He gave short radio talks on how to make backyards and farms appealing to wildlife, such as "Feeding Winter Birds on the Farm." He described conservation as "a way of living on the land." Recruiting Youth Conservation Clubs to work with him, he set up wildlife research areas. "We weren't simply field hands," wrote one member. They were supposed to do

Besides transplanting wild species to the arboretum, Aldo and students use controlled burns to kill off European plant species and bring back the prairie plants.

"deep digging" for facts—"to observe, to ask questions, and to try putting things together." Learning became an exciting and fun adventure.

In January 1934, Aldo began teaching his first class—to a group of young farmers. Shortly after, the president of the United States, Franklin D. Roosevelt, asked him to come to Washington, DC, for a special assignment. Roosevelt had selected Aldo to work with two other conservationists on the President's Committee on Wild Life Restoration. The three members argued briskly over the best methods to use. However, they managed to agree that the government should buy up land for bird sanctuaries and wild-life refuges. They also decided that more scientific research was needed.

In the spring, Aldo took on his first graduate student. In addition, he started planning a university arboretum with other faculty members. Arboretums are usually formal gardens with exotic trees and plants, but Aldo and the committee had something different in mind. They wanted a land laboratory where students could study ecology. There visitors could learn about Wisconsin's original plants and animals. They would even experiment with fire and burning plots of grasses to encourage prairie seeds to grow. Aldo stated: "The time has come for science to busy itself with the earth itself. The first step is to reconstruct a sample of what we had to start with." In this, these professors were pioneering a new science of restoring pieces of land—restoration ecology.

On June 17, 1934, five hundred acres of ruined farmland were dedicated for the University of Wisconsin Arboretum and Wildlife Refuge. Then the real work began. Students and the Civilian Conservation Corps (CCC) labored to rebuild the road. Native trees, wildflowers, and grasses were collected and planted. Grape tangles and brush piles were built up. Wild birds and animals were released on the grounds. Aldo and the other scientists knew that diversity, or a mixture of many different plants and animals, was important for the health of the land. It was the way the lands of Wisconsin used to be.

That summer, rain did not come. Dust storms hurricaned across the plains. The winds moved like carpet sweepers, pulling up soil from fields and tossing it through windows, under doors, into animals' lungs. No one had ever seen anything like it. It was a national disaster. And it had been brought on by poor farming and grazing practices.

Aldo's radio talks boomed in popularity. He was invited to speak on a nationwide radio program. His classes filled up. In Coon Valley, Wisconsin,

Aldo believed conservation requires cooperation, and his Coon Valley project got farmers and university and government specialists working together. The CCC men build a planting terrace over a big gully to stop erosion.

more than 315 farmers signed up to work on a soil, plants, and wildlife restoration project he helped direct. The Soil Erosion Service and CCC men assisted as well, along with Aldo's two eldest sons.

The debate over wilderness protection had not been overlooked either. That fall, a forester named Bob Marshall wrote to Aldo about forming a national conservation group. These "spirited individuals" would fight to preserve the United States' last stretches of wilderness. Marshall asked him to be a leader in this "Wilderness Society." Aldo replied that he was "more than glad to serve."

In January 1935, the day after his forty-eighth birthday, Aldo found something he had been looking for long and hard, a plot of land he could afford to buy for hunting. He came home excited and exuberant about this land along the Wisconsin River. He piled his family into their sedan to go see the treasure. They imagined a nice cabin in the woods with a porch along a beautiful river. All they found were eighty acres of sand, old corn rows, and broken-down fences. In the middle, not far from the river, sat an old chicken coop piled with manure. "When we carry it out and plant it in your garden," Aldo told his wife, "you'll be very glad it was there." She didn't complain, just joined in on this new outdoors adventure. The family nicknamed it "the Shack."

Over the winter months, the kids mucked out the coop and laid down a clay floor. The boys built a wing for sleeping, a new roof, and a handsome fireplace and chimney. They planted sorghum as food for quail and pheasants.

Luna and Estella Jr. are working on adding a wing to the coop for double sleeping bunks. Then the family just took sacks and filled them with hay for mattresses.

Once summer showed its face, Aldo got so busy that the Shack was forgotten. He had been invited to go on a three-month trip to Germany to examine forestry and game-management methods. The tours showed him that Germany's national forests contained little more than the spruce trees planted after logging. They grew in straight rows like soldiers. Deer came to feed at troughs. Pheasants wandered like farm geese. No wolves howled. The forests were as tame as house pets.

Starker finishes the chimney–again! It had to be improved many times to try to keep it from smoking, leaking, and other problems.

The Germans had managed nature so strictly it could no longer work on its own. For game management to be effective, Aldo realized, it had to respect nature and its wildness. The goal could not be to *control* but to *work with* "things natural, wild and free."

Aldo wrote, "Conservation is a state of harmony between man and the land...Harmony with land is like harmony with a friend."

In the spring of 1936, Aldo and his family set to work doing on their own land what they'd been helping with at the arboretum. They were going to re-create their own original Wisconsin. With sharpened shovels, they planted a thousand white pine trees and a thousand red pine. They sunk Juneberry, blackberry, nannyberry, and cranberry bushes into the sandy soil, along with mountain ash, Norway pine, and plum trees.

Nina is at work with her sharpened shovel, planting one of the thousands of pines and other trees and plants the family added each spring and summer to the Shack land.

Everyone worked until they had blisters and backaches. Yet, amazingly, they enjoyed it. When the hot, dry winds came, the plants dried out. The family hauled buckets of water from the river on weekends. Like the rest of the nation's farmers, though, the Leopolds watched most of their plants die. The dust storms kept on coming.

Despite it all, the family noticed a strange affection for the old Shack creeping up on them. Besides the bucket brigades to water their trees, there was always canoeing, swimming, fishing, bird-watching, hunting, studying wildlife, and archery. Estella would bring up cornbread and honey, then relax from cooking. Aldo would take over, cooking in the Dutch oven and organizing the kids with dishes. At night, the guitars came out. The kids would serenade Daddy as he wrote short notes in their Shack Journal.

Throughout that summer, and all summers, Aldo kept up a steady pace at work. Still, he was always firm about weekend trips to the Shack: "Never take anything up there that is not *absolutely* necessary." No radios, gadgets, or fineries. Instead there was a hand pump for water, fishing rods, a shotgun, an ax, shovels, a camera, and a bow and arrow.

The shelves, benches, and outhouse were built out of junk that floated down the river or was

Aldo and Carl wash dishes in the Shack using basins and water from a hand pump outside. On sunny days, the family did dishes with an assembly line on the picnic table.

rescued from the local dump. They added thousands more trees each spring–with even more varieties, including birch, maple, wahoo bush, dogwood, hazel, cedar, and tamarack.

The Leopolds were experimenting with how to live in harmony with a piece of land. They were learning not only to take care of it, but to rebuild it.

And they loved it. It brought them all together and let them each try their own projects. For example, Starker built wildlife shelters. Carl took photographs. Estella rescued prairie flowers to plant at the Shack land. Little Estella sailed toy boats in the river. Together they banded birds, watched the woodcocks dance, and added entries in their Shack Journal.

As the winter of 1936 approached, Aldo took a bow-hunting trip into the Sierra Madre of Mexico. This was a land that was still wild, free, and healthy. It had wolves, jaguars, deer, wild turkeys, thick-billed

The Wisconsin River offered endless delight to the Leopolds. As Estella floats her boat, one can see the outhouse, dubbed the Parthenon, in the field behind her.

At the Shack, Aldo rose before dawn to write and measure the increasing light with the rising birdsong. He also noted the weight, age, and sex of each species he hunted.

parrots, and trout. Aldo had never seen so much wildlife living together in such numbers. "All my life I had seen only sick land," he realized.

This trip sealed the argument for Aldo–the United States must save its last bits of wilderness for science, if for nothing else. Without wild land for comparison, he reasoned, scientists would never be able to diagnose when land was sick. Nor would they ever know what to do to cure it.

# 8

# The Moral of It All

Click, click, click. Everyone knew by the snap of the metal heels against the floor that the professor was coming. He strode into the room, a medium-sized man with a deep voice, a large nose and large ears, and serious, gentle eyes. Aldo's hair was thinning and he wore spectacles, but he still liked a well-cut suit and class tie.

In his course Game Management 118, Aldo led his students out into the fields and woods. There he taught them to read animal and landscape signs and to ask questions, as his father had taught him. One former student said that Professor Leopold "never tired of asking the questions that ended up blowing my mind."

Aldo would take his students out to learn to see the drama in the bush and appreciate outdoors exploration as a sport that could be done even in the city.

Aldo had four graduate students in spring 1937 and about seventy students in his other courses. Things had gotten cramped in the Soils Building. The only space where they could dissect specimens was in the toolshed, on top of a seed drill.

Aldo was content to "make shift with the way things are." But his students were not. One fall night, they posted a guard at the basement door. Then they quietly packed up Aldo's office, his furniture, files, books, paintings, and all.

The next day, when Aldo showed up for work, everything was missing. His students escorted him to 424 Farm Place. It was an old three-story frame house owned by the university. It had a porch, a greenhouse, wooden floors, and a fireplace. As he walked inside, Aldo saw, neatly arranged and waiting for him, all his things.

He was shocked, to say the least, yet pleased. The place soon became quite homey for both the professor and his students. Aldo would rise early in the morning and go there to do his writing. By the time his secretary arrived at eight o'clock, he would have piles of yellow-pad pages to be typed.

In 1938, Aldo began to call himself a professor of wildlife management and renamed his introductory course Wildlife Ecology 118. His job, as he saw it, was "to teach the student to see the land, to understand what he sees, and to enjoy what he understands." He used the word *land* rather than *wildlife*. He felt that it included "all of the things on, over, or in the earth." "Wildlife," he wrote, "cannot be understood without understanding the land." The next year he was made chair of his own university department and budget: the Department of Wildlife Management.

As the 1930s came to a close, Germany, which had tried to control its forests and wildlife, was trying to control the world. One of Germany's allies—Japan—invaded Hawaii on December 7, 1941. The United States entered World War II.

Luna and Carl enlisted. Luna was stationed in the States, and Carl in the war zone. Aldo's courses emptied. For the first time in ages, he had a little time on his hands. He'd been collecting his essays, articles, speeches, journal entries, and scientific field notes over the years. Now he started rewriting them into parts for a single book on the relationship between people and land. The questions he asked were: How could people live on land without spoiling it? And do we have a moral duty to care for it, and the wildlife living with us on the land? If so, what is it?

While working on the book, Aldo was also serving on the Wisconsin Conservation Commission.

The commission faced an ongoing catastrophe. The state's timber wolves had been killed or run off. Because of this, the number of deer had ballooned. The deer were eating up the state's newly planted forests. Where food was scarce, deer were collapsing from starvation and disease.

Part of Aldo's solution was to bring back the wolves. He deeply regretted that he had once worked to kill them off. "I was young then and full of trigger-itch," he wrote. "I thought that because fewer wolves meant more deer, that no wolves would mean hunt-ers' paradise." He hadn't known then how important every species was for a healthy land system. Now he believed each species had an undeniable right to exist.

Most people in Wisconsin refused to have wolves in the state. So the commission voted for a season during which hunters could shoot not only bucks but also does. The result: a slaughter in some areas and few kills in others. Deer lovers lashed out at Aldo, calling him "Bambi Killer."

Aldo had had trouble with his eyes and his health, but now things got worse. He couldn't sleep. He worried about his sons, his students, the deer, the forests, the wolves, the wilderness, and the world in general. When the atomic bomb was dropped on Japan, Aldo was deeply pained. He saw it as a distressing turning point in human history, where people could no longer control their own weapons.

Finally, peace treaties were signed. Carl made it home safely, and his father wept for joy. As the soldiers returned, Aldo was swamped with students. A painful tic developed on one side of his face. When it hit, it was as if he had been "smashed over the head with a sledge hammer."

Aldo tried different methods to heal the problem: rest, less work, and, finally, surgery. But the pain increased. In September 1947, sixty-year-old Aldo traveled to the Mayo Clinic in Rochester, Minnesota, for major surgery. The tic went away, but so did all feeling on the left side of his face. He drooled a little and had trouble concentrating, and his eyes dried quite easily.

Estella and Aldo were doting grandparents, as can be seen with Luna's son, Bruce Carl Leopold, around 1946.

Aldo and Estella had new responsibilities, as grandparents! Both Starker and Luna had married and each had a son. All the while, Aldo tried to fulfill his many responsibilities and get his book of essays published.

Aldo's place of rest and freedom was the Shack. After eleven years, the Leopold land had started to plant itself. Trees spread out above their heads. A prairie bloomed outside their door. Woodcocks danced in the grasses. Only a small patch of sand remained as it had been. Aldo had left "the sand blow" unplanted to tell the land's history.

At the end of February 1948, the US government asked Aldo to be a representative at a United

Carl took this photo of the family relaxing at the Shack in 1939 (clockwise: Aldo, Estella, Luna, Starker, Gus, Estella Jr., and Nina). In the 1940s, the older boys married.

Nations conference on conservation. Aldo had reached the summit of his profession.

Two months later, Aldo received news that Oxford University Press was going to publish his book of essays. He dedicated it to "my Estella."

"There are some who can live without wild things," it began, "and some who cannot. These essays are the delights and dilemmas of one who cannot." The essays described what Aldo had noticed in nature over his lifetime. He explained what these observations had taught him about wildlife, wilderness, ecology, and life. He wrote, "When we see land as a community to which we belong, we may begin to use it with love and respect."

The weekend after Aldo heard from Oxford University Press, he and Estella packed up the car and drove to the Shack to celebrate and relax. Young Stella arrived from college to help sharpen the shovels and plant the trees.

It was Aldo's last spring planting. On Wednesday, April 21, 1948, Aldo Leopold died from a heart attack while fighting a neighbor's grass fire. The *Wisconsin State Journal* wrote, "It is a tragedy...to lose him, his mind, and the good works for which the grandchildren of today's children might thank him."

# Afterword

A *Sand County Almanac*, Aldo's book of essays, was published in 1949. Since then, millions of copies have been sold. The book has been hauled up mountains, trundled into canoes, and stored at bedside tables. It has been translated into Chinese, French, and Russian, as well as other languages. It is one of the best-loved books ever written about the environment.

Aldo left behind more than his books. His children followed in his footsteps and have contributed greatly to the protection of "things natural, wild, and free." His students, and their students, and readers around the world have also carried on his work.

On June 17, 2009, the University of Wisconsin Arboretum and Wildlife Refuge celebrated seventy-five years of growth–three quarters of a century. One could look out and see the kind of forests, wild-grass prairies, and marshes that had once covered Wisconsin.

At the Shack, the trees grow so tall and thick that they have had to be thinned. Rare prairie wildflowers bloom near Aldo's favorite bench. Deer wander past. The old chicken coop has been named a national historic building, and the land is protected as part of the Leopold Memorial Reserve. It remains

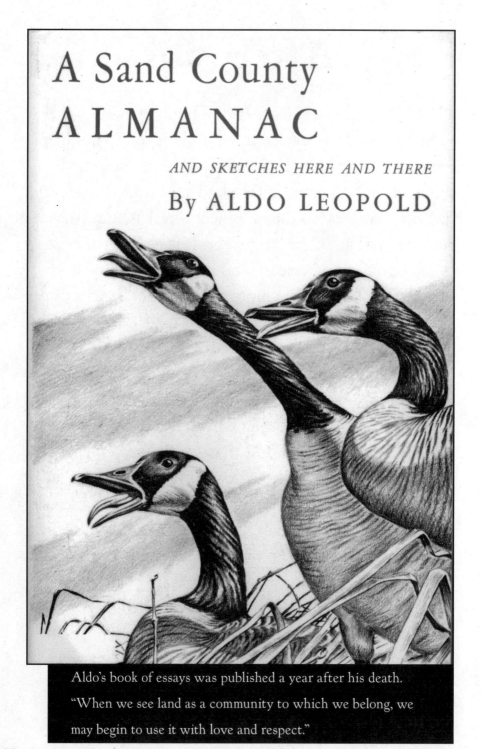

# A Sand County
# ALMANAC

*AND SKETCHES HERE AND THERE*

## By ALDO LEOPOLD

Aldo's book of essays was published a year after his death. "When we see land as a community to which we belong, we may begin to use it with love and respect."

a land laboratory for wildlife managers and students of wildlife ecology. A new, energy-efficient building called the Aldo Leopold Legacy Center has been built on part of the land away from the Shack. Researchers and the public meet there to study the land community and share ideas and findings.

The Shack's replanted woods and prairie grew so wild that a visitor once asked Estella how she and Aldo ever found "such an unmolested corner of natural beauty."

The fight led by Aldo to save US wilderness goes on. Logging, mining, oil drilling, ranching, and building companies demand that no land should be left without wise use. They do not see that land can have its own uses, which are not always clear to us, that we can enjoy.

Some tourists fight to bring snowmobiles, power boats, three-wheelers, and other motorized vehicles into wilderness areas. They don't see the damage motors cause to the soil, water, plants, wildlife, and natural peace. As Aldo would say, "It's enough to make you bite off ten-penny nails."

Aldo's final hope was that people would learn how to read and love the land. He believed that if we love the land, we will do what is right with it.

> I'm trying to teach you that this alphabet of
> "natural objects"(soils and rivers, birds and beasts)
> spells out a story...Once you learn how to read
> the land, I have no fear what you will do to it, or
> with it. And I know many pleasant things it will
> do to you.

He also wrote: "When we see the land as a community to which we belong, we may begin to use it with love and respect." He felt that we need to develop a moral conscience toward the land community. His rule of thumb, or his land ethic, went like this: an action is right if it tends to preserve the health, stability, and beauty of the land community and its natural systems. It is wrong if it tends to do otherwise. And the land community includes people as well as the plants, animals, soil, and water.

It's often tough to know what to do to take care of the land. He wrote, "We shall never achieve harmony with the land, any more than we shall achieve justice or liberty for people." But he added, "In these higher aspirations, the important thing is not to achieve, but to strive."

Aldo lived and wrote, "Harmony with the land is like harmony with a friend."

# US Conservation Time Line

1826–Publication of *The Birds of America* by John James Audubon

1858–First major US city park design for New York's Central Park

1872–First National Park established–Yellowstone

1887–Rand Aldo Leopold born, Burlington, Iowa

1892–Sierra Club founded by John Muir

1902–Publication of *How to Build Up Worn Out Soils* by George Washington Carver

1903–Beginning of National Wildlife Refuge System–Pelican Island, Florida

1905–US Forest Service established

1909–Leopold sent to Apache National Forest, Arizona Territory, for the Forest Service

Aldo at the Apache

1910–Camp Fire Girls and Boy Scouts of America founded

1914–Last known passenger pigeon dies in zoo; four years later, last known Carolina parakeet dies at same place

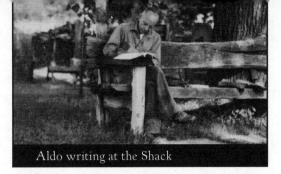
Aldo writing at the Shack

1915–Leopold assigned to Recreation and Game Protection, begins Grand Canyon plan

1923–Leopold's *Watershed Handbook*, the first Forest Service manual on erosion control, published

1924–First US National Wilderness Area, the Gila Wilderness, set aside at Leopold's urging; Leopold moves to Wisconsin to work for Forest Products Laboratory

1933–Leopold's *Game Management* published and he is hired by the University of Wiconisn as the nation's first professor in game management; Civilian Conservation Corps (CCC) created to give young men jobs and conserve natural resources

1935–Leopold cofounds the Wilderness Society and buys the Shack land

1948–Leopold dies, near Madison, Wisconsin

1949–Publication of *A Sand County Almanac* by Aldo Leopold

1962–Publication of *Silent Spring* by Rachel Carson

1964–Wilderness Act

1970–First Earth Day; Clean Air Act; Creation of US Environmental Protection Agency (EPA)

1972–Marine Protection Act

1973–Endangered Species Act

1977–Clean Water Act

2006–The film *An Inconvenient Truth* released on global climate change

2008–Intergovernmental Panel on Climate Change (IPCC) finds global warming trends are largely caused by and can be reduced by human activities

# Glossary

**conservation:** the careful use and protection of natural resources; a way of living in harmony in the land community

**diversity:** a mix of many different animals and plants that live naturally together

**ecology:** the scientific study of animals and plants in relationship with their environment and other species

**environment:** a surrounding area that includes the soils, water, minerals, air, plants, animals, people, and human-made parts

**erosion:** the wearing away of the soil by wind and water

**ethic:** a value and duty to do the right thing

**game animals:** wildlife species that are hunted

**habitat:** the place where an animal or plant naturally lives

**legacy:** something left behind by someone who has died

**predator:** an animal that hunts and eats other animals, such as a wolf

**restoration ecology:** the science of learning to bring back to health a land community or habitat

**species:** a type of living being

**watershed:** the land that surrounds of a body of water such as a lake or river

**wildlife ecology:** the scientific study of the relationships of wildlife species to their habitats and other species in them

**wildlife management:** the human decision to try to guide wildlife species

**wilderness:** an area that has no permanent human-made elements

**woodscraft:** the skills and crafts of living outdoors, especially in the woods

# Places to Visit

## Madison, Wisconsin

- **The Leopold Center.** The Leopold Center is both a headquarters for the Aldo Leopold Foundation and a visitor center for the Aldo Leopold Shack and Farm. Exhibits and signs in the building interpret Aldo Leopold's history and legacy and the green building techniques applied throughout the facility.
- **Aldo Leopold Neighborhood, Aldo Leopold Park, and Aldo Leopold Elementary School.**
- **University of Madison Arboretum, 1207 Seminole Highway.** Visit the Leopold Pines, a forest restoration project planted in the 1930s (some perhaps by Aldo himself) named in honor of his role in developing the arboretum. Also visit the other parts of "the original Wisconsin" he tried to help preserve.
- **Highland Park Neighborhood.** This is where the Leopolds lived, on Van Hise.

## Iowa

- **Aldo Leopold Middle School,** Burlington.
- **Starker-Leopold Historic District,** 101, 111 Clay and 110 Grand streets, Burlington.
- **Starr's Cave Nature Center,** 11627 Starr's Cave Road, Burlington.
- **Black Hawk Cave, Spring, and Trail** and **Crapo Park National Arboretum,** Burlington.
- **Leopold Center for Sustainable Agriculture,** Iowa State University, Ames.

## New Mexico

- Raynold's Neighborhood, Washington Park, Albuquerque. This is the neighborhood where the Leopolds lived, along 14th Street.
- The Aldo Leopold Interpretive Trail and Forest, Rio Grande Valley State Park, Albuquerque. The trail, which starts over a little bridge from the Nature Center, winds through shady cottonwood groves and a restored forest-fire site and has great views of the river and eight interpretive signs about the life of Aldo Leopold.
- Aldo Leopold Wilderness in the Gila Wilderness, near Silver City. Hike where Leopold hiked the Blue Range in the first national wilderness.

## Other Places

- Aldo Leopold Wilderness Research Institute, 790 E. Beckwith, Missoula, Montana.

# Take It Outside

**Start bird feeding and watching.** Create places near you to watch birds and grab a field guide. Then you can count them for science like Aldo did. Join Project FeederWatch, www.birds. cornell.edu/pfw. Your family can also become part of Audubon's annual bird count at Christmastime, http://birds.audubon.org/ get-involved-christmas-bird-count.

**Build a backyard or schoolyard habitat or restore a vacant lot.** Aldo and his family made habitats out of their backyards and then restored the arboretum and Shack lands. You can do the same with others at your home, school, or community. For advice see http://animal.discovery.com/fansites/backyard/ backyard.html.

**Keep an outdoors journal.** Wherever Aldo went, he carried a little notebook and pencil. He got up early to listen to the birds. He also noted the first blooms and birds he saw every spring and the last ones every fall. You can do the same thing. You can even jot down quick notes of the wildlife you see on your cell phone or other device. This is a science called phenology. These records can help you watch for migrating birds and the first signs of spring. You can be part of the Journey North tracking of seasons at www.learner.org/jnorth/KidsJourneyNorth.html. Another phenology Website for kids is http://dnr.wi.gov/org/ caer/ce/eek/nature/season/pheno.asp.

**Map your surroundings.** Aldo loved to tramp along rivers, in the woods and prairies, and make the places his own by making maps and naming the places he found. Seek out your favorite wild places and give it a try. If your family has a GPS, you can mix mapping with the new fun sport of geocaching, a kind of outdoor treasure hunt. To get started, visit www.geocaching.com.

**Become a nature photographer.** Get that camera out and see what moments of amazing adventure and beauty you can capture in nature. Aldo loved to do this, and his son Carl took up the hobby. Take a look at what some kids from Aldo's Wisconsin discovered in this hobby at www.inanewlight.org.

**Sketch wildlife and wilderness.** Aldo learned a great deal about birds by sketching them. Try putting up a bird feeder—then find a comfy spot to watch the birds and sketch them. Or you can draw flowers, grasses, trees, or animals. All you need is a pad of paper and a pencil!

**Plan a wilderness adventure.** Nothing is as cool as leaving behind all the extras of life to try fun, hands-on survival life in the outdoors, like Aldo did. Pick a place you and your family would like to explore on the wilderness map and listings at www.wilderness.net. If your family hasn't done this before, you can work with a wilderness outfitter to get the equipment and tips on how to best enjoy your time. You could even try Leopold's Gila Wilderness or the Boundary Waters/Quetico Canoe Area, which he and his family so loved. (You can even try mapping your trip and assigning personal names to the places you encounter that tell of the experiences you had there.)

**Try a new outdoor activity.** Archery, gardening, fishing, hunting, camping, campfire cooking, and spelunking (cave exploring) were all outdoor hobbies Aldo loved, and you can too! Try to go outside at least an hour a day. For more ideas for outdoors fun, check out www.nwf.org/Get-Outside/Be-Out-There.aspx.

# To Learn More

YouTube presentation on Aldo Leopold and his work, made by a high school student. It has plenty of great photos and won fourth place in Wisconsin in the 2010 National History Day contest. www.youtube.com/watch?v=Wqlp-lteQj4&feature=related

Aldo's daughter Nina Leopold Bradley talking about her father: www.youtube.com/watch?v=9RiKzl9r134&feature=related

The Leopold Education Project has activities and curriculum for teachers who would like to help kids get more involved with the outdoors and encourage a land ethic. www.youtube.com/watch?v=OSotChN0fGk and www.lep.org/about

*Aldo Leopold: A Fierce Green Fire* by Marybeth Lorbiecki. This is a more in-depth book with additional photographs for advanced readers.

*Aldo Leopold's Shack: Nina's Story* by Nancy Nye Hunt, with a foreword by Nina Leopold Bradley. This beautiful and lively then-and-now photo book tells the fun and moving story from Nina's memories of the Leopold family experience on the Shack land–how they built up the chicken coop, played in the river, made music, cooked cornbread, watched animals, and so much more. Readers will really experience how the Leopold's enjoyed their Shack getaway as they brought back the natural habitat and animals together. This is a must-read for anyone interested in Aldo Leopold and his family's experiences at the Shack.

*The Boys' Book of Survival: How to Survive Anything, Anywhere* by Scholastic. The tips and activities in this book work for anyone–certainly not just boys!

*The Dangerous Book for Boys* by Conn Iggulden and Hal Iggulden. This is a book with great adventurous activities for boys *and* girls.

*Earth Matters: An Encyclopedia of Ecology* by DK Publishing

*Ecology* by Brian Lane and Steve Pollock. This book has great facts and photos.

*Ecology Crafts for Kids: 50 Great Ways to Make Friends with Planet Earth* by Bobbe Needham. Here are ways to make things while exploring the outdoors.

*Green Fire* (movie), Aldo Leopold Foundation, US Forest Service, Center for Humans and Nature

*The New 50 Simple Thing Kids Can Do to Save the Earth* by Sophie Javna

*Planet Patrol: A Kids' Action Guide to Earth Care* by Marybeth Lorbiecki. This fun, easy-to-read guide explains the major concepts of the science of ecology with fun facts, activities, photos, and cartoons.

*A Prophet for All Seasons* (movie), NorthWord Press

*The Shape of Betts Meadow: A Wetlands Story* by Meghan Nuttall Sayres. This is the story about restoring a piece of land.

# Major Sources

All quotations have been taken from one of the sources listed below, most often the definitive Meine biography.

Bradley, Nina Leopold. Interview with Marybeth Lorbiecki. July 1991.

———. "Personal Reflections of a Daughter." Unpublished speech, 1991 meeting of the Soil and Water Conservation Society.

Brower, Stephen R. "The Starker-Leopold Family." Research Paper, April 1980, Des Moines County Historical Society.

Flader, Susan L. "Aldo Leopold: A Historical and Philosophical Perspective." Speech, Des Moines County Historical Society, April 17, 1980.

Flader, Susan L., and J. Baird Callicott, eds. *The River of the Mother of God and Other Essays.* Madison: Univ. of Wisconsin Press, 1991.

Gibbons, Boyd. "A Durable Scale of Values." *National Geographic,* November 1981.

Kaufman, Sharon. "Built on Honor to Endure." Speech, Des Moines County Historical Society, September 16, 1986.

Leopold, Aldo. *A Sand County Almanac with Essays on Conservation from Round River.* New York: Ballantine Books, 1990.

Leopold, Frederick. "Recollections of an Old Member [of Crystal Lake Hunt Club]." Speech, March 1977, Crystal Lake Hunt Club, Des Moines County Historical Society.

Leopold Papers: Madison: University of Wisconsin Archives.

McCabe, Robert, ed. *Aldo Leopold: Mentor.* Department of Wildlife Ecology, Univ. of Wisconsin, 1988.

McCabe, Robert. *Aldo Leopold: The Professor.* Amherst, WI: Palmer Publications, 1987.

Meine, Curt. *Aldo Leopold: His Life and Work.* Madison: Univ. of Wisconsin Press, 1988.

Schoenfeld, Clay. "Aldo Leopold Remembered." *Audubon,* March–April, 1978.

Tanner, Thomas, ed. *Aldo Leopold: The Man and the Legacy.* Ankeny, IA: Soil Conservation Society of America, 1987.

Voegeli, Jim. "Remembering Aldo Leopold." Radio documentary, NPR, 1976, 1980, UW Archives.

# About the Aldo Leopold Foundation

The Aldo Leopold Foundation is a not-for-profit organization located near Baraboo, Wisconsin, on the land that inspired Aldo Leopold's classic book *A Sand County Almanac*. Founded by Leopold's children, the foundation works to weave a land ethic into the fabric of our society; to advance the understanding, stewardship, and restoration of land health; and to cultivate leadership for conservation. As owner and manager of the Aldo Leopold Shack and surrounding landscape, the foundation protects the ecological and historical integrity of the site and interprets its importance for thousands of visitors each year. It also curates the vast Aldo Leopold Archives–thousands of documents, photographs, journals, and letters that re-create Leopold's history today. The entire collection is now digitized and is available online. The foundation continues to extend the reach of Leopold's core idea of a land ethic through distribution of *A Sand County Almanac* and the documentary film about Leopold's life and legacy, *Green Fire*. The translation of the book and film into other languages allow Leopold's ideas to reach audiences worldwide. The foundation also works to cultivate future leaders for conservation. Workshops and internships teach sustainable land stewardship and emphasize reflection on humanity's relationship to the land. The foundation is headquartered in the Leopold Center, located less than a mile from the Leopold Shack and Farm. Opened in 2007, the Leopold Center was built using pines the Leopold family planted in the 1930s and '40s and implements a wide spectrum of green building techniques and technologies. The Aldo Leopold Foundation's work to carry forward Aldo Leopold's legacy is membership supported. Learn more about the foundation at www.aldoleopold.org.

# Index